DIGITAL MARKETPLACE

MASTERY

From Newbie to Top-Rated Seller on Fiverr and Beyond

TONI VICTOR BRANT

ISBN: 9798856133065

Dedication

To all the aspiring digital entrepreneurs,

This book is dedicated to your unwavering passion, relentless pursuit of excellence, and boundless creativity. May these pages serve as a guiding light on your journey to top-rated success in the digital marketplace. Your determination and innovative spirit inspire us all. Here's to embracing challenges, seizing opportunities, and leaving an indelible mark in the world of online entrepreneurship.

With heartfelt admiration,

Toni

Contents

Acknowledgments

Congratulations on your journey to becoming a top-rated seller and influential digital entrepreneur. The resources, templates, and insights provided in this book are designed to empower you on your path to success. Remember, your journey is unique, and your impact in the digital marketplace has the potential to be extraordinary. May your days be filled with innovation, growth, and the satisfaction of knowing that your contributions are shaping the digital world for the better.

No journey is undertaken alone, and this book is a testament to the collective effort and support of many individuals. I extend my heartfelt gratitude to:

- My wife, for her unwavering support, encouragement, and understanding throughout the process of creating this guide.

- My mentors and industry peers, whose insights and wisdom have been invaluable in shaping the content and direction of this book.

- The dedicated team who contributed their expertise, time, and enthusiasm to bring this project to fruition.

- The readers and aspiring digital entrepreneurs who inspired me to share my knowledge and experiences in this guide.

Chapter 1

Introduction to Digital Marketplaces

In an era defined by technological innovation and interconnectedness, traditional career paths are undergoing a transformative shift. The rise of digital marketplaces has paved the way for a new paradigm of work, one that empowers individuals to leverage their skills, expertise, and creativity on a global stage. This chapter introduces you to the dynamic world of digital marketplaces, exploring their emergence, significance, and the opportunities they offer to aspiring entrepreneurs.

Section 1.1: The Rise of the Gig Economy

The traditional model of employment, characterized by long-term contracts and fixed working hours, has given way to the gig economy. This shift reflects a broader cultural change where people are seeking flexibility, autonomy, and a diversified income stream. The gig economy is a landscape where temporary and project-based engagements take precedence over traditional full-time jobs. This trend is propelled by several key factors:

Technological Advancements: The proliferation of high-speed internet, smartphones, and digital platforms has made it easier than ever to connect buyers and sellers from different corners of the world. The digital infrastructure allows for seamless communication and collaboration, eliminating geographical barriers.

Changing Work Preferences: Many individuals are drawn to the flexibility and work-life balance that freelancing offers. This trend is further fueled by the desire for greater control over one's time and schedule. Freelancers can choose when, where, and how they work, enabling a more adaptable lifestyle.

Globalization: Digital marketplaces transcend geographical boundaries, enabling professionals to collaborate with clients and customers across international borders. This level of global interaction was previously unimaginable in traditional employment setups.

Section 1.2: The Power of Digital Marketplaces

Digital marketplaces are the epicenter of the gig economy, providing a virtual marketplace where freelancers and clients converge to exchange services and skills. These platforms offer a multitude of advantages:

Access to a Global Customer Base: Digital marketplaces provide an unprecedented opportunity to showcase your offerings to a diverse and extensive clientele. The platform's reach allows you to connect with potential buyers who might never have been accessible through traditional means.

Lower Barrier to Entry: Starting a business or offering services on a digital platform requires significantly less initial investment compared to traditional brick-and-mortar ventures. This reduced financial risk enables more individuals to pursue entrepreneurship.

Streamlined Transactions: Payment processing, communication, and project management tools integrated into digital marketplaces simplify the entire workflow. This efficiency enhances the overall experience for both sellers and buyers.

Meritocracy and Equal Opportunity: Success on digital platforms is often determined by the quality of your work rather than your background. This meritocratic approach levels the playing field and gives everyone, regardless of their background, an equal chance to thrive.

Section 1.3: Exploring Fiverr and Beyond

While a variety of digital marketplaces have emerged, this book shines a spotlight on Fiverr, a pioneering platform that has redefined how individuals monetize their skills. However, the principles and strategies shared throughout this book can be applied to other platforms as well, such as Upwork, Freelancer, and more.

Fiverr: A Pioneer in Digital Freelancing: Fiverr's inception, growth, and unique approach to connecting freelancers and buyers have established it as a leader in the digital marketplace landscape.

Expanding Your Horizon: While Fiverr takes center stage, it's important to recognize that the concepts and techniques covered in this book have universal application. The skills and insights you gain here can be adapted to excel on various digital platforms, broadening your opportunities for success.

As you embark on your journey to become a top-rated seller on Fiverr or any digital marketplace, keep in mind the transformative power of this new era of work. The subsequent chapters will equip you with the knowledge, tools, and strategies to navigate this landscape successfully, positioning yourself as a sought-after professional in the digital realm.

Section 1.4: Embracing the Digital Entrepreneurial Spirit

The digital marketplace revolution isn't merely about exchanging services for money; it's a gateway to embracing the entrepreneurial spirit in its purest form. As a digital entrepreneur, you have the autonomy to shape your business, the creativity to innovate, and the resilience to overcome challenges. This section explores the qualities that define a successful digital entrepreneur:

Adaptability: The ever-evolving nature of digital marketplaces demands the ability to adapt to changing trends, technologies, and customer preferences. Successful digital entrepreneurs are quick learners who embrace change and turn it into an advantage.

Innovation: Creativity knows no bounds in the digital world. Entrepreneurs on digital platforms can explore novel ways to package their services, experiment with new formats, and continuously find ways to stand out.

Problem-Solving: Digital entrepreneurs encounter a diverse range of clients and projects, each with its own set of challenges. The ability to analyze problems and devise effective solutions is a hallmark of a successful seller.

Resilience: The journey to becoming a top-rated seller is not without its setbacks. Resilience is key when faced with rejection, competition, or unforeseen obstacles. A determined digital entrepreneur doesn't let setbacks define their path.

Section 1.5: Your Path to Success

Becoming a top-rated seller on Fiverr or any digital marketplace requires dedication, strategy, and a willingness to learn. While the landscape offers remarkable opportunities, success is not guaranteed overnight. Rather, it's a journey that requires careful planning and consistent effort. In the chapters that follow, you'll delve into actionable strategies and practical advice that will empower you to achieve your goals.

Navigating the Book: To make the most of this guide, approach each chapter as a building block in your journey. From selecting your niche and crafting compelling gig listings to optimizing your profile and delivering exceptional service, every aspect is interconnected and contributes to your overall success.

Unlocking Your Potential: Remember, the digital marketplace is a realm where your potential knows no boundaries. Your success is defined by your willingness to innovate, your commitment to excellence, and your ability to connect with clients in a meaningful way.

As you continue reading, envision yourself not just as a seller on a digital platform, but as a digital entrepreneur equipped with the knowledge and insights to excel. Your journey has begun, and the possibilities are limitless. Let's embark on this path together and uncover the strategies that will lead you to becoming a top-rated seller on Fiverr or any digital marketplace.

This concludes the first chapter of "DIGITAL MARKETPLACE MASTERY." In the chapters that follow, we'll delve into the practical steps and strategies that will guide you towards achieving your goal of becoming a thriving and sought-after digital entrepreneur.

Chapter 2

Niche Selection and Service Offerings

In the expansive landscape of digital marketplaces, finding your niche is akin to discovering your unique identity amidst a bustling crowd. Your niche is not only a reflection of your skills and expertise but also a compass that guides your journey towards success. This chapter delves deep into the art and science of niche selection, helping you carve a distinctive path that resonates with both your passion and market demand.

Section 2.1: Unleashing Your Expertise

Before you embark on your journey to conquer the digital marketplace, take a moment to introspect. What are your strengths? What are you truly passionate about? Your journey begins by recognizing your unique blend of skills, experiences, and interests:

Self-Assessment: Engage in a thoughtful self-assessment to uncover your strengths, skills, and areas of expertise. Consider your educational background, work experience, and personal interests that set you apart.

Passion and Purpose: Explore your passions and discover areas that truly ignite your enthusiasm. Passion fuels creativity and resilience, and it's a key ingredient in creating services that stand out.

Leveraging Your Background: Your life experiences, hobbies, and background can offer unique insights and angles that differentiate you from others. Think broadly about how your background can be a valuable asset.

Section 2.2: Researching Profitable Niches

While passion is a driving force, success in the digital marketplace is also influenced by market demand. Conducting thorough research is essential to identify niches that offer a balance between your passion and financial potential:

Market Trends and Demand: Investigate market trends, emerging industries, and evolving customer needs. Look for niches with a growing demand that aligns with your skills.

Competition Analysis: Study your potential competitors within the niche. Analyze their offerings, pricing, and customer reviews to identify gaps and opportunities for differentiation.

Customer Persona: Develop a clear understanding of your ideal customer persona. What challenges do they face? What solutions are they seeking? Crafting services tailored to your target audience enhances your chances of success.

Section 2.3: Defining Your Unique Selling Proposition (USP)

In a bustling marketplace, a unique selling proposition (USP) is your beacon of differentiation. It's what sets you apart and makes customers choose you over others. Craft a compelling USP that communicates your value effectively:

Distinctive Offering: Define what makes your services unique. Is it your approach, speed, quality, or a specific skillset? Your USP should be a promise that resonates with your target audience.

Solving Customer Pain Points: Address specific pain points or challenges your potential customers are facing. Position yourself as the solution to their problems.

Communicating Value: Craft a concise and powerful statement that encapsulates your USP. Your USP should be prominent in your profile, gig listings, and interactions with clients.

Section 2.4: Choosing Your Service Offerings

With your niche and USP in place, it's time to translate your expertise into tangible service offerings. Clarity and specificity in your offerings not only attract customers but also streamline your workflow:

Service Hierarchy: Organize your services into a clear hierarchy, from basic to premium. This approach allows customers to choose offerings that match their needs and budget.

Package Details: Define the scope of each package, including deliverables, revisions, and add-ons. Transparency builds trust and helps manage customer expectations.

Pricing Strategy: Set competitive and value-based pricing. Consider factors like market rates, complexity of work, and your experience. Price your services to reflect your expertise and the value you provide.

As you embark on the path of niche selection and crafting compelling services, remember that your niche is not a static choice but an evolving journey. The next chapter will guide you through the art of creating an irresistible seller profile that showcases your expertise and captures the attention of potential clients. Your journey to becoming a top-rated seller continues, one step at a time.

Chapter 3

Creating an Irresistible Seller Profile

In the digital marketplace landscape, your seller profile is more than just a virtual business card — it's your opportunity to make a lasting first impression. A well-crafted seller profile conveys professionalism, establishes credibility, and sparks interest in potential buyers. This chapter is dedicated to helping you design a captivating seller profile that stands out from the crowd and compels visitors to explore your offerings further.

Section 3.1: The Visual Impact

In a visually-driven online world, aesthetics matter. Your profile's visual elements are the initial touchpoints that can leave a lasting impact:

Profile Image: Select a high-quality, professional profile image that captures your essence. This could be a clear headshot or an image that represents your niche. Avoid using casual or overly stylized photos.

Cover Photo: Your cover photo should complement your profile image and reflect your brand. It's an opportunity to showcase your creativity and provide a glimpse into your offerings.

Visual Consistency: Maintain a consistent visual theme across your profile image, cover photo, and gig images. Consistency creates a cohesive and memorable impression.

Section 3.2: Crafting Your Profile Description

A compelling profile description is your chance to communicate your story, expertise, and what sets you apart. Craft your description strategically to resonate with potential clients:

Opening Statement: Start with an attention-grabbing opening that communicates your unique value proposition. Use engaging language that captures the reader's interest.

Showcase Expertise: Highlight your skills, experience, and qualifications. Provide a snapshot of your journey and how it aligns with your niche.

Customer-Centric Approach: Address the needs and pain points of your target audience. Explain how your services provide solutions and add value to clients.

Section 3.3: Showcasing Your Portfolio

A well-curated portfolio serves as evidence of your capabilities and helps potential buyers visualize the quality of your work:

Variety and Quality: Include a diverse range of samples that showcase the depth and breadth of your skills. Ensure that each sample reflects your best work and demonstrates your expertise.

Context and Description: Provide context for each portfolio item. Describe the project, your role, challenges you overcame, and the impact of your work on the client's objectives.

Visual Presentation: Present your portfolio items in a visually appealing manner. Use high-resolution images, videos, or interactive elements that allow visitors to engage with your work.

Section 3.4: Highlighting Your Qualifications

Establishing trust is crucial in the digital marketplace. Your qualifications and background play a significant role in building credibility:

Educational Background: Share relevant degrees, certifications, and courses that contribute to your expertise. Highlight how your education aligns with your services.

Work Experience: Detail your professional experience, emphasizing roles that showcase your skills and accomplishments. Use quantifiable achievements to demonstrate your impact.

Awards and Recognition: If applicable, mention any awards, honors, or recognitions you've received in your field. These accolades reinforce your credibility and expertise.

Continual Learning: Demonstrate your commitment to growth by mentioning ongoing learning initiatives, workshops, or industry events you attend to stay updated in your field.

As you refine your seller profile, keep in mind that it's an evolving representation of your journey and expertise. A well-optimized profile not only attracts potential buyers but also lays the foundation for building lasting client relationships. The subsequent chapters will guide you through the process of crafting compelling gig listings, delivering high-quality services, and ultimately, achieving top-rated seller status. Your digital marketplace success story continues to unfold, one profile visit at a time.

Chapter 4

Crafting Gig Listings That Convert

Your gig listings are the virtual shop windows through which potential buyers browse and evaluate your offerings. Crafting compelling gig listings is an art that involves strategic communication, clarity, and persuasion. This chapter is dedicated to helping you create gig listings that not only attract attention but also convert curious visitors into satisfied customers.

Section 4.1: Anatomy of a Successful Gig Listing

Understanding the essential components of a gig listing is fundamental to its effectiveness. A well-structured gig listing comprises key elements that guide potential buyers toward making a decision:

Gig Title: Craft a concise and engaging title that immediately communicates the essence of your service. Use keywords that resonate with your target audience.

Gig Description: Elaborate on your service, its benefits, and the problems it solves. Be clear, concise, and use persuasive language to captivate readers.

Pricing and Packages: Outline the different packages you offer, along with their respective prices and what each package includes. Ensure transparency and provide options for different budgets.

Delivery Time: Clearly state the time it takes to complete the service. Set realistic expectations to avoid any misunderstandings with clients.

Revisions and Add-ons: Specify the number of revisions included in each package and offer additional services (add-ons) that clients can purchase to enhance their experience.

Call-to-Action: Encourage potential buyers to take action by including a clear call-to-action (CTA). This could be a button prompting them to "Contact Me," "Order Now," or "Request a Custom Offer."

Section 4.2: Writing Attention-Grabbing Gig Titles

Your gig title is often the first thing potential buyers see. A captivating title can make the difference between someone clicking on your gig or scrolling past:

Keyword Optimization: Incorporate relevant keywords that potential buyers might use when searching for services like yours. A keyword-rich title improves your gig's discoverability.

Benefit-Oriented Language: Highlight the benefits clients will receive by choosing your service. Address their needs and emphasize the value you offer.

Create Curiosity: Use curiosity-inducing language that prompts potential buyers to explore further. A well-crafted title piques interest and encourages clicks.

Section 4.3: Creating Clear and Concise Gig Descriptions

The gig description is where you provide detailed information about your service, its features, and how it addresses the buyer's needs:

Solution-Oriented Approach: Focus on the solutions your service provides. Describe how your expertise can help clients overcome challenges or achieve their goals.

Showcase Value: Highlight the value clients will receive by choosing your service. Explain the unique aspects that set your offering apart from competitors.

Step-by-Step Explanation: If applicable, outline the process you follow to complete the service. A step-by-step breakdown instills confidence in potential buyers.

Visual Aids: Use bullet points, subheadings, and formatting to make the description easily scannable. Visual aids enhance readability and help buyers quickly grasp the details.

Section 4.4: Setting Competitive Pricing Strategies

Pricing is a delicate balance between reflecting your expertise and appealing to your target audience's budget. A well-considered pricing strategy positions your service competitively:

Market Research: Research similar services within your niche to gauge prevailing market rates. Price your offerings competitively based on industry standards.

Value-Based Pricing: Align your pricing with the value you provide. Clearly communicate how your service justifies the price and offers a high return on investment.

Tiered Packages: Create packages that cater to different needs and budgets. A tiered approach allows buyers to choose an option that aligns with their requirements.

Upsell Opportunities: Structure your pricing to encourage clients to opt for higher-tier packages or purchase add-ons. Upselling can increase the overall value of each transaction.

As you delve into the art of crafting compelling gig listings, remember that each word, detail, and element contributes to the overall impression you make on potential buyers. The next chapters will guide you through the intricacies of delivering exceptional services, building a strong online reputation, and optimizing your presence for search and visibility. Your journey to becoming a top-rated seller unfolds with every well-crafted gig listing, drawing you closer to your goal.

Chapter 5

Delivering High-Quality Services

The cornerstone of success in the digital marketplace is the delivery of exceptional services that not only meet but exceed customer expectations. This chapter is dedicated to helping you master the art of delivering high-quality work, building strong client relationships, and ensuring a seamless and satisfying experience for your buyers.

Section 5.1: Effective Communication and Expectation Management

Clear communication is the foundation of a successful client-seller relationship. Properly managing expectations from the outset helps prevent misunderstandings and ensures a positive experience:

Prompt Responses: Respond to inquiries and messages in a timely manner. Quick communication demonstrates professionalism and dedication to your clients.

Clarify Requirements: Seek clarity on project requirements before starting work. Ask questions to fully understand the client's vision and expectations.

Delivery Timeframes: Set realistic delivery times and communicate them clearly to clients. Be transparent about any potential delays and provide updates if necessary.

Section 5.2: Time Management and Workflow Optimization

Efficiently managing your time and workflow is essential to delivering high-quality services consistently:

Work Breakdown: Divide projects into manageable tasks or milestones. This approach helps you stay organized and ensures steady progress.

Prioritization: Prioritize tasks based on deadlines, complexity, and client preferences. Efficiently allocating your time enhances productivity.

Time Tracking: Utilize time-tracking tools to monitor how long each task takes. Accurate time tracking contributes to accurate pricing and efficient workflow management.

Section 5.3: The Art of Delivering Excellence

Delivering high-quality work goes beyond meeting the basic requirements. Strive for excellence to leave a lasting positive impression:

Attention to Detail: Pay meticulous attention to every aspect of your work, from grammar and formatting to design and functionality.

Value Addition: Go the extra mile by providing additional value to clients. This could include unexpected bonuses, personalized recommendations, or supplementary resources.

Feedback Incorporation: If applicable, incorporate client feedback into your work. Demonstrating your receptiveness to feedback enhances client satisfaction.

Section 5.4: Revisions and Client Satisfaction

Even with meticulous work, revisions may be requested. Handling revisions gracefully is key to maintaining client satisfaction:

Revision Policy: Clearly outline the number of revisions included in each package. Communicate your willingness to make adjustments to ensure client happiness.

Client-Centric Approach: Approach revisions with a client-centric mindset. Emphasize your commitment to meeting their expectations and making necessary improvements.

Timely Revisions: Process revisions promptly to avoid delays in project completion. Timely revisions contribute to overall client satisfaction.

As you embark on your journey to delivering high-quality services, remember that your reputation as a reliable and skilled seller hinges on your ability to consistently exceed client expectations. The subsequent chapters will guide you through strategies for building a strong online reputation, optimizing your presence for search and visibility, and managing your business for long-term success. Each successful delivery propels you closer to becoming a top-rated seller and a trusted name in the digital marketplace.

Chapter 6

Building a Strong Online Reputation

I n the digital marketplace, your reputation is your most valuable asset. A strong online reputation not only attracts potential buyers but also instills confidence and trust in your services. This chapter is dedicated to helping you cultivate and maintain a stellar reputation, handle feedback effectively, and establish yourself as a reliable and reputable seller.

Section 6.1: The Significance of Positive Feedback

Positive feedback is a testament to your professionalism and the quality of your work. It's a powerful tool for building credibility and attracting new clients:

Strive for Excellence: Consistently deliver exceptional work to earn positive feedback. Aim to exceed client expectations with every project.

Customer-Centric Approach: Prioritize client satisfaction and actively seek feedback. A customer-centric approach demonstrates your commitment to their needs.

Impact of Reviews: Positive reviews contribute to higher rankings in search results and increased visibility, leading to more opportunities.

Section 6.2: Strategies for Earning 5-Star Reviews

Earning 5-star reviews requires a combination of delivering outstanding work and providing exceptional customer service:

Clear Communication: Maintain open and transparent communication throughout the project. Address any concerns promptly and proactively.

Exceed Expectations: Go above and beyond to surprise and delight clients. Delivering more than they anticipate enhances the likelihood of receiving glowing reviews.

Personalization: Tailor your approach to each client's unique needs and preferences. Personalization shows that you value their business.

Section 6.3: Addressing Negative Feedback Professionally

Negative feedback is an inevitable part of business, but how you handle it can significantly impact your reputation:

Stay Calm and Professional: Respond to negative feedback calmly and professionally. Avoid becoming defensive or engaging in confrontations.

Apologize and Take Responsibility: If you've made a mistake, acknowledge it and apologize. Taking responsibility demonstrates integrity and a commitment to improvement.

Offer Solutions: Propose practical solutions to address the client's concerns. Whether it's a revision, additional work, or a partial refund, focus on resolving the issue.

Section 6.4: Leveraging Social Proof and Testimonials

Social proof, in the form of testimonials and endorsements, enhances your credibility and reassures potential buyers:

Request Testimonials: Reach out to satisfied clients and request their permission to use their feedback as testimonials. Testimonials provide firsthand accounts of your quality and reliability.

Showcase Past Success: Feature positive feedback prominently on your profile and gig listings. Highlight specific outcomes and benefits that clients have experienced.

Collaborate with Influencers: If applicable, collaborate with influencers or industry experts to provide endorsements. Influencer partnerships can boost your visibility and credibility.

As you navigate the terrain of building a strong online reputation, remember that each positive interaction contributes to your overall image. The next chapters will guide you through optimizing your presence for search and visibility, managing your time effectively, and cultivating customer loyalty. Your reputation is a reflection of your dedication, and with every step, you're inching closer to your goal of becoming a top-rated seller and a trusted name in the digital marketplace.

Chapter 7

Optimizing Your Presence
for Search and Visibility

In the vast digital marketplace, visibility is key to attracting potential buyers and standing out from the competition. This chapter is dedicated to helping you optimize your presence, enhance your discoverability, and leverage digital marketing strategies to reach a broader audience.

Section 7.1: Understanding Search Algorithms

Understanding how search algorithms work on digital platforms is crucial for improving your visibility:

Keyword Research: Identify relevant keywords that potential buyers are likely to use when searching for services like yours. Incorporate these keywords strategically in your profile, gig titles, and descriptions.

Algorithm Factors: Familiarize yourself with the factors that algorithms consider, such as completion rate, response time, and positive reviews. Maintain high standards to align with algorithm preferences.

Constant Learning: Stay updated on platform algorithm changes and best practices. Continuous learning helps you adapt and optimize your approach for better visibility.

Section 7.2: Crafting SEO-Optimized Gig Listings

Search engine optimization (SEO) techniques can significantly enhance the visibility of your gig listings:

Keyword Integration: Incorporate targeted keywords naturally in your gig titles, descriptions, and tags. Avoid keyword stuffing, which can negatively impact readability.

Meta Descriptions: Write compelling meta descriptions for your gig listings. These concise summaries appear in search results and influence click-through rates.

Use of Tags: Choose relevant tags that accurately represent your services. Tags improve the likelihood of your gigs appearing in relevant search queries.

Section 7.3: Leveraging Social Media and Online Presence

Your online presence extends beyond the digital marketplace. Leveraging social media and other online platforms can amplify your visibility:

Social Media Engagement: Engage with potential clients on social media platforms relevant to your niche. Share valuable content, showcase your work, and interact with your audience.

Blogging and Content Creation: Establish yourself as an industry expert by creating blog posts, articles, or videos related to your niche. Valuable content can drive traffic and establish your credibility.

Networking: Participate in online forums, groups, or communities related to your field. Networking allows you to connect with potential clients and showcase your expertise.

Section 7.4: Paid Advertising and Promotions

Paid advertising can provide a targeted boost to your visibility and reach:

Platform Ad Campaigns: Consider investing in platform-specific advertising campaigns to increase the visibility of your gigs. Set clear goals and monitor the effectiveness of your campaigns.

Strategic Promotions: Offer limited-time promotions or discounts to attract new clients and encourage repeat business. Promotions can create a sense of urgency and entice potential buyers.

Influencer Collaborations: Collaborate with influencers in your niche to promote your services. Influencer endorsements can introduce your offerings to a wider audience.

As you explore the realm of optimizing your presence for search and visibility, remember that a well-rounded approach involves a combination of strategic tactics and consistent effort. The next chapters will guide you through effective time management, customer loyalty cultivation, and business growth strategies. With each optimization, you're elevating your digital presence and moving closer to becoming a top-rated seller and a recognized name in the digital marketplace.

Chapter 8

Effective Time Management
and Productivity

I n the fast-paced world of digital marketplaces, mastering time management and productivity is essential for maintaining a thriving business. This chapter is dedicated to helping you optimize your workflow, manage your time effectively, and strike a balance between delivering quality work and managing your business responsibilities.

Section 8.1: The Art of Time Blocking

Time blocking is a technique that involves scheduling specific blocks of time for different tasks:

Prioritization: Identify your most important tasks and allocate focused time blocks for them. Prioritize activities that directly contribute to revenue and client satisfaction.

Task Segmentation: Divide your tasks into categories such as client work, administration, marketing, and skill improvement. Allocate dedicated blocks for each category.

Flexible Adaptation: While time blocking provides structure, be flexible in adapting your schedule based on unexpected circumstances or urgent client requests.

Section 8.2: Efficient Task Management and Tools

Effectively managing your tasks and utilizing productivity tools can streamline your workflow:

Task Lists: Maintain a comprehensive task list to keep track of assignments, deadlines, and priorities. Use digital tools or apps for easy organization and access.

Project Management Tools: Explore project management platforms that help you track tasks, collaborate with clients, and monitor progress.

Automation Tools: Leverage automation tools for routine tasks such as invoicing, reminders, and follow-up emails. Automation frees up your time for higher-value activities.

Section 8.3: Setting Realistic Goals

Setting realistic goals is instrumental in maintaining your focus and measuring your progress:

SMART Goals: Set Specific, Measurable, Achievable, Relevant, and Time-Bound (SMART) goals. Clear goals provide direction and motivate you to stay on track.

Long-Term and Short-Term Goals: Define both long-term aspirations and short-term milestones. Long-term goals guide your overall vision, while short-term goals provide actionable steps.

Regular Evaluation: Periodically assess your progress toward your goals. Adjust your strategies based on your achievements and challenges.

Section 8.4: Managing Client Relationships Effectively

Efficient client management contributes to smooth operations and client satisfaction:

Clear Communication: Maintain open lines of communication with clients. Set expectations, provide progress updates, and promptly address any concerns.

Client Onboarding: Develop a streamlined onboarding process for new clients. Clearly outline project details, timelines, and deliverables to prevent misunderstandings.

Client Relationship Management (CRM): Consider using a CRM system to organize client information, interactions, and project details. A CRM helps you provide personalized service and maintain a positive client relationship.

As you dive into the world of effective time management and productivity, remember that mastering these skills empowers you to navigate the demands of the digital marketplace with confidence. The next chapters will guide you through cultivating customer loyalty, scaling your business, and achieving the coveted status of a top-rated seller. With each well-managed task, you're not only optimizing your workflow but also solidifying your path to becoming a trusted and sought-after professional in the digital marketplace.

Chapter 9

Cultivating Customer Loyalty

In the competitive landscape of digital marketplaces, fostering customer loyalty is a strategic advantage that sets you apart. This chapter is dedicated to helping you build strong and lasting relationships with your clients, ensuring repeat business, referrals, and a loyal customer base.

Section 9.1: Personalized Customer Experiences

Creating personalized experiences for your clients enhances their satisfaction and loyalty:

Tailored Solutions: Customize your services to meet each client's unique needs. Address their specific challenges and goals to demonstrate your dedication.

Personalized Communication: Use clients' names and reference their project details in your communications. Personalization shows that you value their business.

Follow-Up and Check-Ins: After project completion, follow up with clients to ensure their satisfaction. Regular check-ins build rapport and show that you care about their success.

Section 9.2: Providing Exceptional Customer Service

Exceptional customer service is a cornerstone of cultivating loyalty:

Prompt Responses: Respond promptly to client inquiries, messages, and concerns. Quick communication instills confidence and shows professionalism.

Going the Extra Mile: Anticipate client needs and exceed expectations whenever possible. Small gestures can leave a lasting positive impression.

Problem Resolution: Handle issues or concerns with empathy and efficiency. A quick and effective resolution showcases your commitment to client satisfaction.

Section 9.3: Rewarding Loyalty

Acknowledging and rewarding loyal clients reinforces their commitment to your services:

Exclusive Offers: Offer special discounts, promotions, or packages to loyal clients. Exclusive benefits show your appreciation for their continued support.

Referral Programs: Implement a referral program that rewards clients for referring new business to you. Referral incentives encourage clients to actively promote your services.

Loyalty Programs: Consider a loyalty program where clients earn rewards or benefits based on the frequency or value of their purchases.

Section 9.4: Gathering and Utilizing Feedback

Feedback is a valuable resource for understanding your clients' needs and improving your services:

Feedback Requests: Solicit feedback from clients after project completion. Use surveys or direct communication to gather insights into their experience.

Continuous Improvement: Act on feedback to enhance your services. Demonstrating your responsiveness to client suggestions fosters trust and loyalty.

Testimonials and Reviews: With client permission, use positive feedback as testimonials on your profile. Testimonials showcase your track record and build credibility.

As you embark on the journey of cultivating customer loyalty, remember that each satisfied client contributes to the growth and sustainability of your business. The next chapters will guide you through strategies for scaling your business, optimizing your financial management, and achieving the coveted status of a top-rated seller. Your commitment to building strong client relationships is a testament to your dedication and professionalism, propelling you toward becoming a respected name in the digital marketplace.

Chapter 10

Scaling Your Business for Growth

As a successful digital entrepreneur, the potential for growth and expansion is within your reach. This chapter is dedicated to helping you strategize and implement methods to scale your business, reach new heights, and capitalize on the opportunities available in the dynamic world of digital marketplaces.

Section 10.1: Diversifying Your Offerings

Diversification allows you to cater to a broader range of clients and revenue streams:

Expand Service Offerings: Introduce new services or variations of your existing offerings to attract different client segments.

Cross-Selling and Upselling: Cross-sell complementary services to your existing clients. Upselling involves encouraging clients to purchase higher-tier packages or add-ons.

New Niches and Markets: Explore entering new niches or targeting different industries to expand your reach and client base.

Section 10.2: Collaborations and Partnerships

Strategic collaborations and partnerships can accelerate your business growth:

Collaborate with Other Sellers: Partner with sellers offering complementary services to offer bundled packages or joint promotions.

Affiliate Partnerships: Establish affiliate relationships where other individuals or businesses promote your services in exchange for a commission.

Industry Influencers: Collaborate with influencers or thought leaders in your industry to extend your reach and credibility.

Section 10.3: Hiring and Outsourcing

As your business expands, consider delegating tasks through hiring or outsourcing:

Virtual Assistants: Hire virtual assistants to handle administrative tasks, client communication, and project coordination.

Freelancers and Contractors: Outsource specialized tasks to freelancers or contractors, allowing you to focus on core activities.

Focus on Core Competencies: Delegate tasks outside your expertise to professionals, allowing you to concentrate on delivering high-quality work.

Section 10.4: Scaling Through Automation

Leveraging automation tools can streamline your operations and enable growth:

Automated Workflows: Set up automated workflows for repetitive tasks such as client onboarding, follow-up emails, and project updates.

Financial Management: Use automation to manage invoicing, payment reminders, and expense tracking.

Analytics and Reporting: Utilize automated analytics tools to track performance, identify trends, and make informed business decisions.

As you explore strategies for scaling your business, remember that growth requires careful planning, resource allocation, and continuous adaptation. The next chapters will guide you through optimizing your financial management, preparing for long-term success, and achieving the prestigious status of a top-rated seller. With each strategic step, you're edging closer to establishing a thriving and influential presence in the digital marketplace.

Chapter 11

Financial Management and Sustainability

E ffective financial management is a cornerstone of a sustainable and thriving digital business. This chapter is dedicated to helping you navigate the financial aspects of your entrepreneurial journey, from budgeting and pricing strategies to managing cash flow and ensuring long-term financial sustainability.

Section 11.1: Pricing Strategies for Profitability

Setting the right prices is essential for achieving sustainable profitability:

Value-Based Pricing: Price your services based on the value you provide to clients. Clearly communicate how your offerings address their needs and deliver a return on investment.

Cost Analysis: Calculate the costs involved in delivering your services, including your time, tools, and overhead. Ensure your prices cover these costs while providing a reasonable profit margin.

Competitive Analysis: Research market rates and competitor pricing to position your services competitively while reflecting your expertise.

Section 11.2: Budgeting and Expense Management

Creating a budget and managing expenses help you maintain financial stability:

Budget Planning: Develop a budget that outlines your expected income, expenses, and savings goals. Allocate funds for business growth and personal needs.

Expense Tracking: Monitor your expenses closely to identify areas where you can reduce costs or optimize spending.

Emergency Fund: Build an emergency fund to cover unexpected expenses or downturns in your business. Having a financial safety net is crucial for long-term sustainability.

Section 11.3: Cash Flow Optimization

Maintaining healthy cash flow is vital for sustaining your business operations:

Invoicing and Payment Terms: Clearly define your invoicing terms and payment schedules. Encourage timely payments to ensure a consistent cash flow.

Payment Methods: Offer a variety of payment options to accommodate clients' preferences and reduce payment delays.

Account Receivables Management: Monitor outstanding payments and follow up on overdue invoices promptly.

Section 11.4: Tax Planning and Compliance

Proper tax planning and compliance are crucial for avoiding financial pitfalls:

Tax Deductions: Familiarize yourself with tax deductions and credits available to freelancers and digital entrepreneurs. Deductible expenses can lower your tax liability.

Record Keeping: Maintain accurate financial records, including income, expenses, and receipts. Organized records simplify tax filing and financial analysis.

Professional Advice: Consult with a tax professional or accountant to ensure you're meeting your tax obligations and maximizing your financial benefits.

As you navigate the realm of financial management and sustainability, remember that a well-balanced approach to pricing, budgeting, and cash flow is essential for achieving long-term success. The next chapters will guide you through preparing for top-rated seller status, mastering customer satisfaction, and making your mark as a reputable and influential digital entrepreneur. With each financial decision, you're building the foundation for a thriving and enduring business in the digital marketplace.

Chapter 12

Preparing for Top-Rated Seller Status

Achieving top-rated seller status is a significant milestone that reflects your dedication to excellence and client satisfaction. This chapter is dedicated to helping you understand the criteria for top-rated seller status, preparing your business for the application, and maximizing the benefits of this prestigious recognition.

Section 12.1: Understanding Top-Rated Seller Criteria

Top-rated seller status is typically awarded based on a combination of factors:

Completion Rate: Maintain a high completion rate by delivering on-time, quality work and avoiding cancellations.

Response Rate: Respond promptly to client inquiries and messages to demonstrate your commitment to communication.

Customer Satisfaction: Receive consistently positive reviews and high ratings from satisfied clients.

Sales Volume: Achieve a certain level of sales volume to showcase your success in the marketplace.

Section 12.2: Optimizing Your Profile and Gigs

Enhancing your profile and gig listings contributes to your eligibility for top-rated seller status:

Profile Updates: Ensure your profile is complete, up-to-date, and accurately reflects your skills, expertise, and offerings.

Gig Quality: Continuously improve the quality of your services, portfolio, and descriptions to attract positive attention.

Buyer Requests: Respond to buyer requests in a professional and timely manner, showcasing your dedication to meeting client needs.

Section 12.3: Delivering Consistent Excellence

Consistency is key in achieving top-rated seller status:

Quality Control: Implement rigorous quality control measures to ensure every project meets or exceeds client expectations.

Client Communication: Maintain open and effective communication throughout each project, addressing client needs and concerns promptly.

Timely Delivery: Strive to deliver work on or before deadlines, demonstrating your reliability and professionalism.

Section 12.4: Showcasing Your Achievements

When you meet the criteria for top-rated seller status, it's important to showcase your achievements:

Prominent Badge: Display the top-rated seller badge prominently on your profile to build credibility and attract more clients.

Updated Portfolio: Continuously update your portfolio with your best work to demonstrate your skills and expertise.

Client Testimonials: Encourage satisfied clients to leave testimonials and reviews that highlight your exceptional service.

As you prepare for top-rated seller status, remember that consistency, client satisfaction, and continuous improvement are your allies in achieving this esteemed recognition. The next chapters will guide you through mastering customer satisfaction, becoming a thought leader in your industry, and leaving a lasting impact on the digital marketplace. Your journey to becoming a top-rated seller is a testament to your hard work, dedication, and commitment to excellence.

Chapter 13

Mastering Customer Satisfaction

C ustomer satisfaction is not only a goal but a continuous journey that defines your success in the digital marketplace. This chapter is dedicated to helping you go beyond meeting expectations and delighting your clients, ensuring that each interaction leaves a positive and lasting impression.

Section 13.1: Building Lasting Relationships

Fostering lasting client relationships is the foundation of customer satisfaction:

Personalization: Address clients by their names and remember their preferences. Personalization creates a sense of connection and importance.

Regular Updates: Keep clients informed about project progress, milestones, and any developments. Transparent communication builds trust.

Exceed Expectations: Consistently go above and beyond to deliver more than what clients expect. Surpassing expectations leaves a memorable impact.

Section 13.2: Active Listening and Empathy

Listening to clients and understanding their needs is essential for providing tailored solutions:

Active Listening: Pay close attention to clients' requirements and concerns. Ask clarifying questions to ensure you fully grasp their expectations.

Empathetic Approach: Put yourself in the client's shoes and demonstrate empathy. Understanding their perspective enhances client satisfaction.

Custom Solutions: Craft your services to specifically address clients' pain points and objectives. Tailored solutions showcase your commitment to their success.

Section 13.3: Seamless Communication

Smooth and efficient communication enhances the overall customer experience:

Response Time: Respond promptly to messages and inquiries, even if it's a simple acknowledgment. Prompt responses show professionalism and attentiveness.

Clarity and Transparency: Clearly convey project details, timelines, and deliverables. Transparent communication prevents misunderstandings.

Accessible Channels: Provide multiple communication channels, such as email, messaging apps, and video calls, to accommodate clients' preferences.

Section 13.4: Anticipating and Solving Problems

Proactively addressing challenges demonstrates your commitment to client satisfaction:

Problem Prevention: Identify potential issues before they arise and take preventive measures. Addressing problems preemptively minimizes disruptions.

Timely Solutions: If problems do occur, resolve them swiftly and effectively. Prompt solutions minimize client stress and showcase your reliability.

Learning from Mistakes: Use each challenge as an opportunity to learn and improve. Demonstrating growth and adaptability reinforces client trust.

As you embark on the journey of mastering customer satisfaction, remember that every delighted client becomes an ambassador for your services. The next chapters will guide you through becoming a thought leader in your industry, optimizing your online presence, and achieving lasting success as a top-rated seller. With each satisfied customer, you're not only building a thriving business but also leaving a positive mark on the digital marketplace.

Chapter 14

Becoming a Thought Leader

Positioning yourself as a thought leader in your industry elevates your status and influence in the digital marketplace. This chapter is dedicated to helping you establish your expertise, share valuable insights, and inspire trust and respect within your niche.

Section 14.1: Sharing Knowledge Through Content

Creating and sharing valuable content showcases your expertise and provides value to your audience:

Blogging: Maintain a blog where you share industry insights, tips, and trends. Consistent blogging establishes you as a knowledgeable resource.

Video Content: Produce informative videos or tutorials related to your niche. Video content engages audiences and demonstrates your expertise visually.

Ebooks and Guides: Write comprehensive ebooks or guides that address common challenges in your industry. Offer these resources as valuable downloads.

Section 14.2: Public Speaking and Webinars

Participating in public speaking engagements and webinars enhances your visibility:

Webinar Hosting: Conduct webinars on topics relevant to your expertise. Webinars allow you to engage directly with your audience and showcase your knowledge.

Guest Speaking: Seek opportunities to be a guest speaker at industry events, conferences, or podcasts. Speaking engagements enhance your credibility.

Panel Discussions: Participate in panel discussions where you can share your insights alongside other industry experts.

Section 14.3: Networking and Collaboration

Building relationships with fellow professionals strengthens your position as a thought leader:

Industry Networking: Attend industry events, conferences, and online forums to connect with peers and share your expertise.

Collaborate with Experts: Partner with other thought leaders or influencers on joint projects or content. Collaborations expand your reach and credibility.

Mentorship: Offer mentorship or coaching services to newcomers in your field. Sharing your expertise helps others while showcasing your knowledge.

Section 14.4: Consistent Online Presence

Maintaining a consistent online presence reinforces your position as a thought leader:

Social Media Engagement: Regularly share valuable insights, articles, and updates on your social media profiles.

Respond to Trends: Stay current with industry trends and provide your unique perspective on relevant developments.

Q&A Sessions: Host Q&A sessions on social media or online platforms to directly interact with your audience and address their questions.

As you strive to become a thought leader, remember that consistent and valuable contributions to your industry set you apart as a respected authority. The next chapters will guide you through optimizing your online presence, managing your business for long-term success, and achieving the prestigious status of a top-rated seller. With each insightful piece of content, you're not only building your personal brand but also leaving an indelible mark on the digital marketplace.

Chapter 15

Optimizing Your Online Presence

Your online presence is your digital storefront, and optimizing it is crucial for attracting and retaining clients. This chapter is dedicated to helping you enhance your visibility, engage your audience, and create a compelling online brand that resonates with potential buyers.

Section 15.1: Crafting a Compelling Profile

Your profile is often the first impression clients have of you. Make it memorable:

Professional Bio: Write a concise yet impactful bio that highlights your expertise, experience, and unique selling points.

High-Quality Photo: Use a professional and friendly profile photo that reflects your personality and professionalism.

Portfolio Showcase: Curate a portfolio showcasing your best work. Visual examples demonstrate your capabilities effectively.

Section 15.2: Engaging Content Creation

Create content that captivates your audience and showcases your expertise:**Valuable Blog Posts**: Consistently write blog posts or articles that address industry challenges, trends, and solutions.

Visual Content: Share visually appealing content, such as infographics, videos, or animations, to convey information creatively.

Engaging Social Media Posts: Craft engaging posts on social media platforms that encourage interaction and discussion.

Section 15.3: Active Social Media Engagement

Engaging with your audience on social media platforms enhances your online presence:

Regular Updates: Post updates and content consistently to keep your audience engaged and informed.

Respond to Comments: Engage with comments and messages promptly, fostering a sense of community and approachability.

Thoughtful Sharing: Share valuable insights, industry news, and relevant content to position yourself as an industry authority.

Section 15.4: Building an Email List

An email list is a powerful tool for staying connected with your audience:

Offer Valuable Incentives: Provide valuable resources, such as ebooks, guides, or templates, in exchange for email sign-ups.

Regular Newsletters: Send regular newsletters that include updates, valuable content, and offers to keep your audience engaged.

Personalized Communication: Segment your email list and tailor your communications to specific audience interests and needs.

As you focus on optimizing your online presence, remember that consistency, engagement, and authenticity are key to attracting and retaining clients. The next chapters will guide you through effective time management, long-term business success, and achieving the prestigious status of a top-rated seller. With each online interaction, you're not only enhancing your visibility but also shaping your identity as a respected figure in the digital marketplace.

Chapter 16

Long-Term Business Success

A chieving long-term success in the digital marketplace requires strategic planning, adaptability, and a focus on continuous improvement. This chapter is dedicated to helping you navigate the challenges and opportunities that come with sustaining a thriving digital business over the years.

Section 16.1: Goal Setting and Vision

Setting clear goals and maintaining a long-term vision are fundamental to sustained success:

Define Your Vision: Outline your long-term vision for your business, including where you want to be in the next 1, 5, and 10 years.

SMART Goals: Set Specific, Measurable, Achievable, Relevant, and Time-Bound (SMART) goals that align with your vision.

Regular Review: Periodically assess your progress toward your goals and adjust your strategies as needed.

Section 16.2: Continuous Learning and Skill Development

Staying current with industry trends and enhancing your skills is vital for long-term success:

Learning Opportunities: Attend workshops, webinars, and conferences to expand your knowledge and stay updated on industry developments.

Skill Enhancement: Continuously improve your skills and adapt to emerging technologies or changes in your field.

Networking and Collaboration: Connect with other professionals to exchange insights and stay informed about industry advancements.

Section 16.3: Adapting to Market Changes

The digital marketplace is dynamic, and adaptability is essential:

Market Research: Stay informed about market trends, shifts in demand, and emerging opportunities.

Pivot Strategies: Be prepared to adjust your offerings or strategies in response to changing market conditions.

Customer Feedback: Listen to your clients' feedback and be willing to make changes based on their evolving needs.

Section 16.4: Building a Resilient Mindset

Developing resilience helps you navigate challenges and setbacks:

Positive Outlook: Maintain a positive and optimistic attitude, even in the face of challenges.

Problem-Solving Skills: Cultivate strong problem-solving skills to address obstacles effectively.

Self-Care: Prioritize self-care to manage stress and maintain your mental and physical well-being.

As you work toward long-term business success, remember that adaptability, resilience, and a commitment to growth are key ingredients. The next chapters will guide you through effective time management, achieving financial stability, and attaining the prestigious status of a top-rated seller. With each strategic decision, you're not only building a thriving business but also shaping a legacy of accomplishment in the digital marketplace.

Chapter 17

Achieving Financial Stability

Maintaining strong financial health is essential for the sustainability and growth of your digital business. This chapter is dedicated to helping you manage your finances, make informed decisions, and ensure the long-term financial stability of your entrepreneurial journey.

Section 17.1: Smart Financial Planning

Effective financial planning is the cornerstone of financial stability:

Budgeting: Create a detailed budget that outlines your income, expenses, and savings goals. Stick to your budget to avoid overspending.

Emergency Fund: Build and maintain an emergency fund to cover unexpected expenses or periods of low income.

Savings and Investments: Allocate a portion of your earnings to savings accounts or investments to secure your financial future.

Section 17.2: Profit Margin Optimization

Maximizing your profit margins is crucial for sustainable growth:

Cost Analysis: Regularly assess your expenses and identify areas where you can reduce costs without compromising quality.

Pricing Strategy: Continuously evaluate your pricing strategy to ensure it aligns with market rates and covers your costs.

Value-Added Services: Consider offering premium or value-added services that command higher prices and increase your profit margins.

Section 17.3: Effective Invoicing and Payment Management

Efficient invoicing and payment management contribute to steady cash flow:

Professional Invoices: Create clear and professional invoices that detail the scope of work, payment terms, and due dates.

Payment Options: Offer multiple payment methods to accommodate clients' preferences and facilitate prompt payments.

Payment Terms: Clearly communicate your payment terms and follow up on overdue payments promptly.

Section 17.4: Tax Planning and Compliance

Navigating tax obligations is essential for financial stability:

Tax Deductions: Familiarize yourself with tax deductions and credits applicable to your business. Deductible expenses reduce your tax liability.

Quarterly Payments: If required, make quarterly estimated tax payments to avoid penalties and manage your tax obligations.

Professional Assistance: Consult with a tax professional or accountant to ensure accurate tax reporting and compliance.

As you work toward achieving financial stability, remember that effective financial management is a continuous process that requires diligence and careful planning. The next chapters will guide you through strategies for achieving the prestigious status of a top-rated seller, leaving a lasting impact in the digital marketplace, and solidifying your position as a respected industry professional. With each financial decision, you're not only securing your business's future but also establishing a legacy of success in the digital landscape.

Chapter 18

Reaching Top-Rated Seller Status

Attaining top-rated seller status is a culmination of your dedication, expertise, and exceptional service. This chapter is dedicated to guiding you through the final steps towards achieving this prestigious recognition, solidifying your reputation as a top performer in the digital marketplace.

Section 18.1: Consistent Excellence

Consistency is key to achieving and maintaining top-rated seller status:

Quality Control: Maintain consistently high-quality work and deliver exceptional value to each client.

Communication: Prioritize open and transparent communication to ensure client satisfaction and prevent misunderstandings.

Timely Delivery: Strive to meet or exceed project deadlines, demonstrating reliability and professionalism.

Section 18.2: Soliciting Positive Feedback and Reviews

Positive feedback and reviews play a crucial role in your journey to top-rated seller status:

Request Reviews: Politely ask satisfied clients to leave positive reviews and testimonials on your profile.

Provide Guidance: Offer clear instructions on how clients can leave reviews and share their feedback.

Client Satisfaction: Continuously focus on exceeding client expectations to naturally generate positive reviews.

Section 18.3: Managing Disputes and Challenges

Navigating disputes and challenges with professionalism is essential:

Resolution Efforts: Make earnest efforts to resolve any issues or conflicts with clients in a fair and amicable manner.

Customer Service: Demonstrate exceptional customer service, even in challenging situations, to preserve client satisfaction.

Learning Opportunities: Treat challenges as learning opportunities to improve your processes and prevent similar issues in the future.

Section 18.4: Maintaining Eligibility

Sustaining top-rated seller status requires ongoing commitment:

Regular Evaluation: Continuously assess your performance metrics to ensure you meet the eligibility criteria.

Adaptability: Stay updated on platform changes and adjust your strategies as needed to align with evolving requirements.

Continuous Improvement: Strive for continuous improvement in your services, communication, and client interactions.

As you embark on the final steps toward top-rated seller status, remember that your dedication to excellence and client satisfaction has brought you to this point. The next chapter will guide you through solidifying your reputation and leaving a lasting impact in the digital marketplace as a respected top-rated seller. Your journey is a testament to your hard work, professionalism, and commitment to success.

Chapter 19

Leaving a Lasting Impact

B ecoming a top-rated seller is not the end of your journey; it's a stepping stone toward leaving a lasting impact in the digital marketplace. This chapter is dedicated to helping you create a legacy of influence, inspire others, and contribute to the growth and development of your industry.

Section 19.1: Mentorship and Sharing Knowledge

Passing on your knowledge and expertise contributes to the growth of aspiring entrepreneurs:

Mentorship Programs: Establish mentorship programs or offer guidance to newcomers in your field.

Educational Resources: Create and share educational resources, guides, or workshops that empower others to succeed.

Open Communication: Encourage open communication and collaboration within your industry to foster a supportive community.

Section 19.2: Thought Leadership

Continue your journey as a thought leader to inspire and guide others:

Thoughtful Content: Create thought-provoking and insightful content that challenges norms and encourages innovation.

Industry Advocacy: Advocate for positive changes and advancements within your industry to drive growth and progress.

Conference Speaking: Participate in industry conferences as a keynote speaker to share your insights and experiences.

Section 19.3: Giving Back and Social Impact

Using your success for social impact adds depth to your legacy:

Charitable Initiatives: Support charitable causes or initiatives that align with your values and contribute to positive change.

Community Engagement: Engage with your local or online community through volunteering, donations, or awareness campaigns.

Positive Influence: Use your platform to promote ethical practices, sustainability, and social responsibility within your industry.

Section 19.4: Continuous Growth and Evolution

Your journey doesn't end with top-rated seller status; it's a foundation for ongoing growth:

Skill Enhancement: Keep improving your skills, staying abreast of industry trends, and evolving with changing demands.

Innovation: Embrace innovation and new technologies to stay relevant and push boundaries in your field.

Long-Term Vision: Continue setting ambitious goals and working toward your long-term vision for your business and industry.

As you focus on leaving a lasting impact, remember that your influence extends beyond your individual success. By sharing your knowledge, inspiring others, and contributing to positive change, you're shaping the future of the digital marketplace and leaving a legacy that goes beyond transactions—it's about transformation, inspiration, and lasting change.

Chapter 20

Your Journey Forward

Congratulations! You've reached the final chapter of this book, but your journey as a top-rated seller and influential digital entrepreneur is just beginning. This chapter is dedicated to offering you guidance as you move forward, reminding you of the key principles that will continue to propel your success.

Section 20.1: Embracing Continuous Learning

Never stop learning and growing:

Stay Curious: Maintain a curious mindset and stay open to new ideas, technologies, and opportunities.

Seek Feedback: Welcome constructive feedback as a tool for improvement and growth.

Adaptability: Embrace change and be adaptable in the ever-evolving landscape of the digital marketplace.

Section 20.2: Building Resilience

Resilience will sustain you through challenges:

Mindset Matters: Cultivate a resilient mindset that sees obstacles as stepping stones to success.

Learn from Setbacks: Each setback is a chance to learn, adapt, and come back stronger.

Self-Care: Prioritize self-care to maintain your physical, mental, and emotional well-being.

Section 20.3: Fostering Relationships

Nurture your relationships with clients and peers:

Client Relationships: Continue delivering exceptional value and building strong client connections.

Collaborations: Seek opportunities for collaborations that can expand your reach and impact.

Networking: Engage in networking to stay connected with industry trends and fellow professionals.

Section 20.4: Setting New Goals

Keep setting goals to fuel your progress:

Dream Big: Set audacious goals that inspire you and align with your long-term vision.

Measure and Adjust: Regularly measure your progress and adjust your strategies to stay on course.

Celebrate Achievements: Acknowledge and celebrate your accomplishments, both big and small.

Section 20.5: Your Impactful Journey

Your journey as a top-rated seller and influential digital entrepreneur is a testament to your dedication, hard work, and determination. Remember that you're not just selling services—you're making a difference in the lives of your clients, your industry, and the digital marketplace as a whole.

As you step into the future, carry with you the lessons, insights, and principles from this book. Your journey forward is filled with limitless possibilities, and your role as a top-rated seller is an integral part of shaping the digital landscape and inspiring others. Embrace each challenge and opportunity, and continue leaving your mark as a true leader in the world of digital entrepreneurship. Your journey is one of impact, growth, and enduring success.

Conclusion

A Digital Entrepreneur's Odyssey

As we conclude this book, it's important to reflect on the incredible journey you've embarked upon as a digital entrepreneur striving for top-rated seller status. Your path has been marked by dedication, innovation, and a commitment to excellence. You've learned how to navigate the intricacies of digital marketplaces, cultivate customer loyalty, and position yourself as a thought leader in your industry. You've discovered the art of effective communication, optimized your online presence, and honed your financial management skills. Along the way, you've not only achieved top-rated seller status but also left a lasting impact on the digital landscape.

Remember that your journey is ongoing, and the principles and strategies outlined in this book are your compass for the road ahead. As you continue to evolve, adapt, and learn, your influence will extend beyond transactions to transformation. Your legacy will be defined by the positive changes you bring to your industry, the lives you touch, and the inspiration you provide to fellow digital entrepreneurs.

In the dynamic and ever-changing world of digital marketplaces, your success as a top-rated seller is a testament to your ability to navigate challenges, seize opportunities, and embrace growth. The digital marketplace is your canvas, and you, the artist, have the power to create, innovate, and leave an indelible mark.

As you move forward, remember that you have the tools, knowledge, and determination to continue shaping your destiny as a respected, influential, and prosperous digital entrepreneur. Your journey is an odyssey filled with promise, potential, and the fulfillment of your aspirations. Go forth with confidence, creativity, and a passion to make your mark on the digital world. Your story has just begun, and the possibilities are boundless.

Thank you for embarking on this journey with us, and we wish you every success in your continued pursuit of excellence and impact in the digital marketplace.

Resources and Tools

In your journey to becoming a top-rated seller and successful digital entrepreneur, having access to the right resources and tools is crucial. Here are some recommended resources to support your growth and enhance your skills:

1. **Online Learning Platforms**: Platforms like Coursera, Udemy, and LinkedIn Learning offer a wide range of courses on topics such as digital marketing, business management, communication, and more.

2. **Project Management Tools**: Tools like Asana, Trello, or Monday.com can help you streamline your project management, keep track of tasks, and meet deadlines.

3. **Financial Management Software**: Consider using tools like QuickBooks, FreshBooks, or Wave for efficient invoicing, expense tracking, and financial reporting.

4. **Graphic Design Tools**: Create stunning visuals and graphics for your online presence using tools like Canva, Adobe Spark, or Piktochart.

5. **Communication and Collaboration Tools**: Platforms like Slack, Microsoft Teams, or Zoom can facilitate seamless communication and collaboration with clients and peers.

6. **Social Media Management Tools**: Use tools like Hootsuite, Buffer, or Later to schedule and manage your social media posts across different platforms.

7. **Website and Portfolio Builders**: Platforms like WordPress, Wix, or Squarespace allow you to build professional websites and portfolios to showcase your work.

8. **Industry Blogs and Publications**: Stay updated on industry trends and insights by following blogs, publications, and forums related to your niche.

9. **Networking Events and Conferences**: Attend virtual or in-person industry events, webinars, and conferences to connect with peers and learn from experts.

Top-Rated Seller Checklist

- ☐ Use this checklist as a quick reference to ensure you're meeting the criteria for top-rated seller status:
- ☐ Maintain a high completion rate by delivering projects on time and avoiding cancellations.
- ☐ Respond promptly to client messages and inquiries to maintain a high response rate.
- ☐ Focus on delivering exceptional quality to receive consistently positive reviews and high ratings.
- ☐ Achieve a certain level of sales volume to demonstrate your success in the marketplace.

Goal Setting Template

Setting goals is essential for your ongoing success. Use this template to define your goals, strategies, and action steps:

Goal: State your specific goal!

_____

_____

Strategies: Outline your strategies for achieving the goal!

1. _____

2. _____

3. _____

Action Steps: List the specific steps you need to take to implement each strategy!

1. _____

2. _____

3. _____

4. _____

5. _____

Reflection Journal

Use this journal to reflect on your journey, track your progress, and set intentions for the future:

Date: _____

Reflections: Record your thoughts, experiences, and insights from the day!

_____

_____

_____

_____

_____

Goals for Tomorrow: List your goals and intentions for the next day!

_____

_____

_____

_____

Recommended Reading List

Expand your knowledge and perspective with these recommended books that can further enhance your skills and mindset as a top-rated seller and digital entrepreneur:

1. "The Lean Startup" by Eric Ries

2. "Influence: The Psychology of Persuasion" by Robert B. Cialdini

3. "Good to Great" by Jim Collins

4. "Atomic Habits" by James Clear

5. "Deep Work" by Cal Newport

6. "Crushing It!: How Great Entrepreneurs Build Their Business and Influence—and How You Can, Too" by Gary Vaynerchuk

7. "The Art of Possibility" by Rosamund Stone Zander and Benjamin Zander

8. "Dare to Lead: Brave Work. Tough Conversations. Whole Hearts." by Brené Brown

9. "Purple Cow: Transform Your Business by Being Remarkable" by Seth Godin

10. "Start with Why: How Great Leaders Inspire Everyone to Take Action" by Simon Sinek

Glossary of Key Terms

Enhance your understanding of key terms and concepts related to digital entrepreneurship, top-rated seller status, and the digital marketplace:

1. **Conversion Rate**: The percentage of website visitors or users who take a desired action, such as making a purchase or signing up for a newsletter.

2. **Lead Magnet**: An incentive or valuable resource offered to potential clients in exchange for their contact information.

3. **ROI (Return on Investment)**: The ratio of net profit to the initial cost of an investment, often used to measure the effectiveness of marketing campaigns.

4. **Niche**: A specialized segment of a larger market, focusing on a specific area of expertise or interest.

5. **Elevator Pitch**: A concise and compelling description of your services or business that can be delivered in the time it takes to ride an elevator.

6. **CTA (Call to Action)**: A prompt or instruction that encourages users to take a specific action, such as clicking a button or making a purchase.

7. **Brand Identity**: The visual and verbal elements that define your brand, including logo, colors, typography, and messaging.

8. **A/B Testing**: Comparing two versions of a webpage, email, or advertisement to determine which one performs better in terms of engagement or conversion.

9. **SEO (Search Engine Optimization)**: Strategies and techniques to improve a website's visibility on search engines, leading to higher organic (unpaid) traffic.

10. **Analytics**: The collection, measurement, and analysis of data to gain insights into user behavior and improve decision-making.

Frequently Asked Questions (FAQ)

Here are answers to some common questions that digital entrepreneurs often have as they strive to become top-rated sellers and excel in the digital marketplace:

Q1: How long does it take to become a top-rated seller? A: The time it takes to achieve top-rated seller status can vary based on factors such as your niche, the quality of your work, and your level of client satisfaction. Consistency and dedication are key.

Q2: What should I do if I receive a negative review? A: Address the situation professionally and courteously. Reach out to the client to understand their concerns and offer a resolution. Future positive reviews will outweigh occasional negatives.

Q3: How can I manage my time effectively as a digital entrepreneur? A: Set clear priorities, create a schedule, and use time management tools. Delegate tasks when possible and take breaks to avoid burnout.

Q4: What's the best way to handle difficult clients or disputes? A: Approach the situation calmly and professionally. Communicate openly, seek solutions, and be willing to compromise. Document all interactions for reference if needed.

Q5: How can I stand out in a competitive digital marketplace? A: Focus on delivering exceptional quality, excellent customer service, and effective communication. Offer unique value and build a strong personal brand.

Q6: How important is networking for my digital business? A: Networking is crucial for building relationships, learning from peers, and accessing new opportunities. Engage in online and offline networking events to expand your reach.

Q7: What strategies can I use to handle periods of low income? A: During lean times, focus on marketing efforts, diversifying your services, or seeking short-term projects. Use the time to improve your skills and refine your offerings.

Q8: How can I maintain motivation and avoid burnout? A: Set realistic goals, take regular breaks, practice self-care, and celebrate small wins. Surround yourself with a supportive community of peers.

Permissions, Copyright and Notices

For permissions, inquiries, or to report copyright infringement, please contact:

Email: toni.v.brant@gmail.com

Please note that while this book provides valuable insights and strategies, I cannot guarantee that its content will lead every reader to become a top-rated seller. Success on digital marketplaces like Fiverr depends on a variety of factors, including individual effort, market conditions, and competition. However, the knowledge and guidance presented here can significantly enhance your understanding and approach toward achieving top-rated seller status.

Additional Resources

Expand your knowledge and skills further with these additional resources that can support your journey as a top-rated seller and digital entrepreneur:

1. **Podcasts**: Listen to podcasts on entrepreneurship, digital marketing, and business growth to gain insights and stay updated on industry trends.

2. **Online Communities**: Join online forums, groups, or communities related to your niche to connect with like-minded individuals, ask questions, and share experiences.

3. **Industry Reports**: Stay informed about industry trends and data through reports published by relevant organizations or research firms.

4. **Webinars and Workshops**: Participate in webinars and workshops hosted by industry experts to learn new strategies and techniques.

5. **Ebooks and Whitepapers**: Access ebooks and whitepapers on topics such as marketing, branding, and business development.

6. **Coaching and Mentoring**: Consider working with a business coach or mentor who can provide personalized guidance and support.

7. **Advanced Courses**: Explore advanced courses that delve deeper into specific aspects of digital entrepreneurship, such as advanced SEO, social media advertising, or advanced financial management.

Quick Tips Reference

A compilation of quick tips and reminders to help you stay focused, productive, and effective as you navigate your journey as a top-rated seller and digital entrepreneur.

1. **Clear Communication**: Effective communication is the cornerstone of successful client relationships. Be clear, concise, and prompt in your messages.

2. **Quality Over Quantity**: Prioritize delivering high-quality work over taking on too many projects. Excellence will set you apart.

3. **Continuous Learning**: Embrace a growth mindset and commit to continuous learning. Stay updated on industry trends and best practices.

4. **Client-Centric Approach**: Always put the client's needs and satisfaction first. Tailor your services to meet their specific requirements.

5. **Feedback Loop**: Regularly seek feedback from clients to improve your services and address any concerns promptly.

6. **Time Management**: Use time management techniques to prioritize tasks, set realistic deadlines, and avoid burnout.

7. **Networking**: Build a strong network of peers, mentors, and industry professionals to exchange ideas and opportunities.

8. **Financial Planning**: Manage your finances wisely by budgeting, saving, and investing for long-term stability.

9. **Personal Branding**: Craft a compelling personal brand that reflects your expertise, values, and unique selling points.

10. **Resilience**: Develop a resilient mindset to navigate challenges and setbacks with determination and positivity.

About the Author

Toni V. Brant is a seasoned digital entrepreneur with 12 years of experience in the digital marketplace. With a passion for voice acting and recording, Toni has successfully navigated the challenges and opportunities of the digital landscape, achieving top-rated seller status and establishing a reputation as a thought leader in the industry.

Toni is committed to sharing knowledge, empowering fellow entrepreneurs, and making a positive impact in the digital marketplace. Through his journey, Toni continues to inspire others to excel, innovate, and thrive in the dynamic world of digital entrepreneurship.

Stay connected with the author and access additional resources through the following channels:

Email: toni.v.brant@gmail.com

Author's Website: www.youtube.com/@ToniVBrant

Reader Feedback

Your feedback is invaluable in helping us improve and provide you with the best resources. We would love to hear your thoughts on this book. Please feel free to share your feedback, suggestions, and any topics you'd like to see covered in future editions.

You can reach us at:

Email: toni.v.brant@gmail.com

Thank you for taking the time to share your insights with us. Your input contributes to the ongoing growth and refinement of this guide.

Once again, thank you for joining us on this journey of becoming a top-rated seller and influential digital entrepreneur. Your commitment to excellence, innovation, and growth is what sets you apart in the digital marketplace. As you move forward, may your path be filled with endless opportunities, meaningful connections, and a legacy that shines brightly in the digital landscape. Here's to your continued success and impact in the dynamic world of digital entrepreneurship

www.ingramcontent.com/pod-product-compliance
Lightning Source LLC
Chambersburg PA
CBHW062356290526
45794CB00005B/2253